In 1909 an up Deeside Express charges across the moor hauled by a highly-polished Great North of Scotland Class T No.104. GNS engines were always beautifully turned out.

Introduction

ROYAL DEESIDE! Wonderful country with farms, forests and moorland running from the sea at Aberdeen to the high mountains above Braemar — to say nothing of salmon fishing and attractive towns and villages.

Today's visitors can see all this within about two hours driving time but it was not always so easy. It was the need to open up the country to trade that led to the building of the railway on Deeside — and what a railway it was. Always within sight of river or mountain and indeed for much of the journey, both at the same time.

Many of the stations were in keeping with their surroundings. Banchory and Aboyne of fitting stature for the towns they served; Torphins and Lumphanan attractive in their own right; Ballater with its Royal waiting room built for Queen Victoria — but the real accolade must go to tiny Cambus O'May perched on a narrow shelf just above the river. The stationmaster could almost catch his breakfast fish lying in his bed!

Perhaps fortunately for visitors the curves and gradients kept speed down. Not for them being rushed through at 125 mph, with no opportunity to savour the scenery. They could watch a fisherman playing his salmon, or the farmer and forester at work. It was all very friendly.

Today it is difficult to realise that all this was possible from the comfort of a railway train because sadly it came to an end in 1966, when the passenger service stopped running.

Hopefully this booklet will give today's visitor something of the story and character of a railway journey they can no longer enjoy.

Dick Jackson
June 1994

Front cover: **A quiet morning at Ballater station from the days prior to the Great War as the engine crew of No.14 pause for the camera of Sir Malcolm Barclay-Harvey.**

Back cover: **Diesel days at Banchory Dee Street. In 1961, it became the first new station on Deeside this century. A mere five years later the line was closed.**

The Deeside Railway

THE valley of the River Dee has been a trade route linking the North-east Highlands with Aberdeen and the coast for many generations. By the late 17th century early tracks and footpaths had developed into a well used pack-horse road, parts of which are still in use, little altered apart from modern surfacing. The most obvious sections are to be found on the minor road linking Bridge of Canny and Kincardine O'Neil and also the pass of Ballater road. There are also the remains of a small bridge in a garden to the west of Crathie Church. Such a road could not carry the timber that was sent to the coast from the large areas of forest in the valley, and huge quantities were floated down the river until well into the 19th century. It was inevitable, therefore, that there would be proposals to build a railway running inland from Aberdeen.

September 1845 saw the first meeting of the promoters of a railway to go at least as far as Banchory and prospects seemed favourable. The Deeside Railway Act received the Royal Assent on 16th July 1846 but, as with so many other proposals at that time, financial problems arose and the first turf was not cut until 5th July 1852. There were no great construction problems and the railway opened to Banchory on 8th September 1853.

To start with the Aberdeen terminus was at Ferryhill about $^1/_2$ mile south of the present station and was shared with the Aberdeen Railway which connected the city with the south. Later a new joint station was built more or less on the site of the present goods depot before both railways finally moved to the present location in 1867.

The line from Banchory to Ballater was constructed by two nominally separate companies. The Deeside Extension Railway was opened to Aboyne on 2nd December 1859 with the final section to Ballater being undertaken by the Aboyne and Braemar Railway. Thus, on 17th October 1866 it was at last possible to make the entire journey to Aberdeen by train. As its name implies, the Aboyne and Braemar Company had intended to go right through to Braemar and indeed the track was laid on the short length from Ballater to Bridge of Gairn, but did not survive for long. Queen Victoria did not relish the prospect of trains passing close to Balmoral even though they would have been on the other side of the river, so third party influence was brought to bear which put an end to the proposal. All three Companies were worked by the Deeside Railway, which was the only one with any rolling stock.

The trackbed at Bridge of Gairn

While there had been no doubt about the projected route of the line between Ferryhill and Banchory, there were differing opinions from there on. The direct route to Aboyne via Kincardine O'Neil was held to be easier to build and work, especially as it would have avoided the steep gradients on the line as constructed. What is more, several of the influential landlords were ready to support the proposal. However the route through Torphins carried the day and Kincardine O'Neil faded into oblivion until rescued by the coming of motor vehicles. Torphins, on the other hand, flourished and from a state of virtual non-existence prior to the advent of the railway, it developed into a popular summer resort. Beyond Aboyne, a line through Coull and Tarland in the fertile Cromar was suggested as being more remunerative but in the event the route crossing Muir of Dinnet was adopted. Thus Tarland was left in a similar plight to that of Kincardine O'Neil.

The generally easy nature of the countryside meant there were no great engineering difficulties to overcome. The only large viaduct, with five masonry arches, crossed the Beltie Burn about one mile west of Torphins. A short distance further on, the line entered a very deep rock cutting known locally as 'Satan's Den' which was to become the scene of frequent snow blocks. Just west of Aboyne station came a short tunnel under part of the village.

One interesting feature still to be seen at Cambus O' May concerns an alteration to the ferryman's house where, in order to provide room for both the railway and road at the narrow defile, one corner of the house had to be removed.

The three Deeside companies continued to have a separate existence until the Great North of Scotland Railway leased them all on 1st September 1866 for a period of 999 years. Complete

The ferryman's house at Cambus O'May

amalgamation followed nine years later and the line settled down to life as a branch, albeit an important one, of its new owner. It was always physically separated from the rest of the Company's system by the short section of track out to Ferryhill Junction owned by the Caledonian Railway, as successor to the Aberdeen Railway. It was not until the formation of British Railways in 1948 that the whole came under one ownership. In the meantime, of course, the GNSR had itself lost its identity in 1923, becoming part of the new London and North Eastern Railway.

Locomotives

The original intention was for the Aberdeen Railway to work the Deeside Railway but it was unable to provide sufficient locomotives and vehicles to give a reasonable service and the Deeside set about acquiring its own rolling stock.

Eight engines were bought between 1854 and 1866; all carried a livery of dark blue with black lining which was kept in magnificent condition. Seven of the locomotives were sturdy 0-4-2s built by Messrs Hawthorn of Leith. One had an interesting history, having been built for the Banffshire Railway, and passing to the GNSR when they took that company over in 1863. It was later sold to the Deeside and so eventually returned to the Great North. The eighth was a poor thing from the Rotherham works of Messrs Dodds & Co and was spurned by the GNSR when they came on the scene. For all that, an anonymous writer to 'Engineering' had this to say about the Hawthorn engines —

> On the occasions when the royal train goes over the line, the speed is higher than for ordinary traffic. We are certain that engines of this construction would not be considered safe for fast trains on the main lines in the south of England, and we wish to ask whether they are reckoned perfectly safe for exceptionally high speeds

upon the crooked and undulating line which partly occupies the distance between Aberdeen and Balmoral.

As the trains had an average speed of about 20mph it is tempting to ask the meaning of "exceptionally high speed"! When the Great North leased the three Companies it was a condition that the Deeside stock retained its own numbers. This was too much for that Company's Locomotive Superintendant, William Cowan, who found himself with eight Deeside engines having the same numbers as his own so he promptly did the sensible thing and re-numbered the lot.

All these engines had been withdrawn by 1883 and the trains were then worked by Great North engines which were mainly moderately-sized 4-4-0s. The first 'foreign' engines were seen when the LNER brought some ex-North British Railway 4-4-0s of Class D31 to Aberdeen during the 1920s. Later still saw the arrival of real strangers in the shape of former Great Eastern Railway 4-6-0s of Class B12, although at first they were not allowed to work beyond Banchory. The final year of LNER ownership brought the Class B1 4-6-0, these being the first brand new engines in the area for over 25 years. As in 1923, so in 1948 the arrival of British Railways at first saw the status quo continue, but the new owner's standard engines could be seen from the early 1950s until steam finally disappeared in 1961.

Until 1958 all the trains were steam hauled. In that year not only did the usual diesel railcars appear on the passenger trains but also an experimental electric railcar powered by batteries which were re-charged at Aberdeen and Ballater. Unfortunately this interesting unit did not live up to its early promise and was withdrawn from public use in 1962 although it was later restored privately and is at present (1994) working on the East Lancs Railway, north of Manchester.

The battery railcar at Dinnet

Train Services

When opened to Banchory in 1853, there were three return trains every weekday, taking about an hour for the journey. After extension to Ballater there were four passenger trains each way daily which took between $2^1/_2$ and 3 hours to cover the 43 miles. The service gradually built up to its peak just before the Great War when there were seven Ballater trains, one of them an express, as well as four locals going as far as Banchory, with extras running on Wednesdays and Saturdays. By then the time to Ballater was around $1^1/_2$ hours and even the latter day diesel railcars hardly bettered that. An interesting development in 1914 was the introduction of a slip-coach at Banchory. This was a method of providing a service at a station without the train having to stop; the guard using a special mechanism to uncouple the slip coach from the moving train. In this case it was dropped off the 4.45pm to Ballater but it was short-lived as the Great War intervened and it was not re-instated afterwards. This is believed to be the only example of a slip-coach operating on a standard gauge single track line.

At the Aberdeen end of the line an intensive suburban service started in 1894 over the first seven miles out to Culter. Some eighteen trains were added to the basic Deeside service and these covered the distance in 21 minutes including eight stops — even BR's electric trains are hard pushed to beat that! Gradually bus, car and tram competition built up and the 'Subbies' as these trains were known, were withdrawn in 1937.

A Local 'Derby'

A down 'Subbie' at Cults

The historic Railway Race between London and Aberdeen in 1895 when the rival East and West Coast companies vied to reach the Granite City first is well known. Much less well known was the local 'Derby' which could be witnessed almost daily during the 1920s between the Joint Station and Ferryhill Junction. Both the Great North and the Caledonian Railways had trains leaving the south end of the station at 1.00pm.

Sometimes one or other of the trains was delayed in starting and the race was off but more often than not the guards' whistles would sound within moments of each other and the fun would start. Side by side and often on adjacent tracks the two trains would race alongside each other with passengers gazing through the windows at their opposite numbers and frequently exchanging facial and other signs until the Deeside line swept off to the west at Ferryhill Junction. It must be admitted that usually the race took a set form — the GNSR train being by far the lighter would gain an initial advantage and it would seem as if it was going to sweep past its adversary, but once the more powerful Caledonian locomotive got its train really started the lost ground would be made up and faces which you thought, and hoped, would never be seen again would reappear, often carrying a hateful grin of triumph, especially if belonging to the younger generation.

Caley (left) and Deeside train at the Joint

The writer recalls one glorious occasion when the Caledonian train was headed by a much larger engine than the usual McIntosh 'Dunalastair' III or IV and one which positively dwarfed the GNSR engine. This time the Caley got away some seconds before the Deeside train and it looked as if it was going to be a 'walk-over' for the opposition. However, the GNSR driver made a splendid start when his turn came and it was evident that he was going to make a fight for it as, quite soon, to the surprise of all concerned, the Deeside train started to make up on its rival which seemed to be making rather heavy weather of it and, passing it in great style, was away off on to the branch line before the Caley could make up on it. The writer can remember to this day the look of disgust on the faces of the Caledonian engine's crew.

(James Irvine in the Great North Review)

The War Years

Along with the rest of the railway system Deeside saw a big reduction in its train service during the 1939-45 war. The Sunday trains which the LNER had introduced as a Summer service in 1928 disappeared and were never restored while only four daily trains were left. Against that, goods traffic increased very considerably, especially in timber from the large areas of forest on Deeside.

Maurice Shand, who was appointed stationmaster at Ballater in 1943, tells of

> an average of 100 wagons of timber per day being forwarded. A large tonnage came from the three Canadian (logging) camps in the district. The station was very busy. Tanks were received and reloaded; commando troops and Indian regiments with pack mules trained in the district. Large quantities of hay and straw were received for the mules, trainloads of which arrived in cattle trucks. Special trains of troops came and went. A new siding was built about half a mile east of Ballater where heavy forwarding of timber took place. Another new siding was also built adjacent to Platform 2 and was known as the Canadians' Bank with very heavy loading of timber there also. The permanent staff was increased by two female clerks and a junior female porter. They all received more pay than I did (£252 p.a.) because I got no overtime and they did. No increase in engine power was given nor in locomotive staff. It was hard going.

In the end over half a million tons of timber were despatched by rail from Deeside.

Excursion Trains

From the very beginning holiday and excursion traffic was expected to form a substantial part of the potential revenue of the railway on Deeside. Indeed, the first excursions were advertised to run only five days after the opening to Banchory.

A fine summer weekend would send the crowds up the valley, but they went by rail and not by car or bus along the present A93. An Aberdeen Holiday Monday in the early years of this century could see some twenty trains going to Banchory of which nine at least went on to Ballater. All this in addition to the usual service of 'Subbies' to Culter. Since the line was single beyond Park and the trains ran from the then notoriously cramped Joint Station there must have been some headaches for the operators! Excursion tickets were certainly value for money as the return fare to Ballater cost 3/- (15p).

One example taken from 1926 shows that on Saturday 16th June no less than 3,285 people, made up from eleven Sunday School parties, went out to Pitfodels, Murtle, Milltimber and Culter. They travelled in three special trains which left Aberdeen between 1.53pm and 2.22pm with the regular 2.05 'Subby' also running. Let us hope the sun shone!

Special trains would also run for such events as the Highland Games at Aboyne and Braemar, to say nothing of those operated into Aberdeen for the Royal Northern Show, football matches and even theatrical events for which the railway would even book seats for travellers. In hard winters Aboyne Loch was used for 'Bonspiels' and a special platform was provided there for the use of curlers.

The Great North always regarded the Deeside Line as one of its main tourist attractions and gave it wide publicity. As an added interest to the journey, in 1918 the height of the line above sea level was shown on station name boards from Banchory onwards. This caught the eye of the LNER Directors when they visited Deeside in 1925 so that the idea was extended to other lines in Scotland with tourist traffic.

In 1933 the LNER introduced Camping Coaches, at first in England and later also north of the border. By 1935 they could be found at Banchory, Crathes and Murtle while later they were also placed at Aboyne, Torphins and Ballater. In fact Banchory proved so popular that two coaches were located there.

Royal Train Journeys

The Royal family bought Balmoral in 1851 and the first Royal journey was undertaken only a month after the opening to Banchory when the Duchess of Kent, Queen Victoria's mother, travelled south from that station on 11th October 1853. Two days later the Queen herself left Balmoral for the south, but due to the atrocious state of the roads arrived in Banchory twenty five minutes late (which was very unusual for her.) From then on, journeys by British and foreign royalty brought much traffic to the Deeside Railway and its successors. As the line was extended these journeys started from Aboyne and then Ballater although Queen Victoria continued to use Aboyne for almost a year after Ballater station was opened.

Conditions there must have been rather primitive, Royal traffic notwithstanding, because in 1884 Mr McKenzie of Glenmuick wrote personally to William Ferguson the Chairman of the GNSR suggesting that a Royal waiting room would be appreciated.

> The expense could only be a trifle for making a small room of the kind required, and would appear as a kindly offer of respect coming unsolicited from the Railway. Should the Railway not have the funds to do so, I have no doubt other Railways drawing advantage from the traffic would gladly contribute although I think you will agree with me that it would look better coming from the Deeside Railway alone if you could manage it, and for this reason I make the letter private to you, that if done it should appear to be the spontaneous action of the Railway.

This prompted (shamed?) the directors into taking action and in 1884 they duly approved the re-building of the station. Included in the plans was a Royal waiting room modelled on that at Wolferton, the station for Sandringham. The new station was opened in 1886 and when the Queen arrived on Saturday 21st August she inspected, and approved, the new Royal waiting room.

A great deal of work was involved in handling the Royal train and its movement would be covered by confidential notices issued to, and signed for by, everybody involved. Precise instructions were given concerning the running of other trains on the route, security at points and level crossings and, not least, ensuring that the train stopped at the exact point where the red carpet had been laid!

GNS Royal train en route to Ballater

The last Royal train on Deeside left Ballater at 7.15pm on 15th October 1965 hauled by two diesel engines. Despite the steady downpour the Queen was seen off by a crowd of two hundred or so people.

As things turned out, that was not to be the last Royal visit to Ballater station. When the reigning King or Queen arrived by train it was usual for them to inspect the Royal Guard drawn up in the square outside. The last time this ceremony had taken place was in 1964, as in 1965 Her Majesty reached Aberdeen by sea and then drove to Balmoral. From time to time there had been suggestions that the ceremony should be revived and the Committee of the Great North of Scotland Railway Association thought that the centenary of the Waiting Room would be a suitable occasion.

Her Majesty graciously approved the suggestion and so when she went to Balmoral on 16th August 1986 arrangements were made for her car to arrive on the platform side of the station, as though she had come by train. There she was met by the Lord Lieutenant of Aberdeenshire, Sir Maitland Mackie together with the only surviving stationmaster of Ballater, Mr Maurice Shand. The Queen then moved out into the square where she inspected the Royal Guard drawn from the 1st Battalion of the Black Watch.

The 'Messenger' Trains

When Queen Victoria began to spend part of each year in Balmoral her despatches had perforce to be sent north daily. At first these came by road from Perth via Blairgowrie and the Cairnwell Pass but in 1865 this arrangement was altered and they came by rail via Aberdeen. The connecting service on to Ballater was provided by a special train known as 'The Queen's Messenger'. To begin with it consisted of a solitary coach for the messenger himself but later a First Class carriage was added for visitors to Balmoral and later still a Third Class for the use of their servants. Eventually the trains appeared on the public timetable. These were the only trains on the Great North system to run on the Sabbath. The Treasury paid for them at the rate of £9:2/- (£9.10) for each return journey, including £1:1:6 (£1.07^1/2) to cover the cost of a carriage and pair to complete delivery to the castle. However by 1887 it seems that the Treasury reckoned that the Great North was charging too much. At all events the Company agreed to reduce the charge to a rate of 1/6 (7^1/2p) per mile with the Treasury paying the cost of 'posting' beyond Ballater. So far as the train was concerned the Treasury thus saved £1:11/- (£1.55) each day it ran. The Messenger trains continued to run until 1937 when the despatches reverted to the original route via Perth and Braemar.

'The Queen's Messenger' led to a lawsuit in 1883. When Crathes station to the east of Banchory was opened, it was a condition that all trains other than those chartered privately would stop there. By 1878 the 'Messengers' were in the public timetable as was a Saturday-only excursion to Banchory, neither of

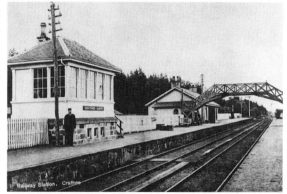

Crathes station, looking towards Aberdeen (M. Appleby)

which stopped at Crathes. Sir Robert Burnett of Leys, who owned Crathes estate, therefore told the Great North that it was in default of its obligations. To cut a long story short the whole dispute ended up in the House of Lords in 1885 as a result of which the 'Messenger' had to stop at Crathes but the excursion was allowed to pass as it was not available to passengers with ordinary tickets! Thereafter all trains duly stopped at that station until in 1914 Sir Robert's successor set aside the relevant clause in the Feu Charter.

The Beginning of the End

Sadly, the Deeside line found disfavour under the Beeching Report and when it was published in 1963 a local committee was formed to oppose withdrawal of services. Because of objections the closure, originally proposed for 2nd March 1964, had to be postponed pending a hearing by the Transport Users Consultative Committee. It was all to no avail and on 31st August 1965 the Minister of Transport decreed that no real hardship would arise from the loss of rail services. Following that, British Railways announced that passenger trains would cease to run from 28th February 1966.

"Tickets please" at Lumphanan (J. Cook)

The last passenger train was the 8.35pm from Aberdeen on Saturday 26th February 1966. Quite a number of people made use of the fact that it had to return to Aberdeen as empty stock to make a last, unofficial, round trip. A large crowd awaited the train's arrival at Ballater and the hostelry on the station did a roaring trade — indeed it was reported that certain liquids had run dry! Mr W. Stewart, the stationmaster, summoned the passengers with the century-old bell and the train left to the usual broadside of detonators. All along the line the lights went out for the last time and an otherwise merry occasion was tinged with sadness at the redundancy of many railwaymen. This final train arrived at Platform 6 in the Joint Station at 11.38pm where two ticket collectors awaited it and then the passengers followed in single file as the Inspector led them out of the station.

So after just over 100 years passengers were no longer able to enjoy this very scenic journey. If the trains had survived a few more years modern signalling systems could have greatly reduced running costs and perhaps we would still be able to see the beautiful scenery from the comfort of a railway carriage.

Goods trains to Ballater lingered on until 18th July of that year when they were cut back to Culter, largely due to the presence of the paper mill in that town. Even then the end was not far off and the very last train on the Deeside line ran on 30th December 1966.

"Farewell Ballater"

The goods train to Ballater on Friday 15th July 1966 was the last to traverse the whole route.

It was a dull, rather damp morning as I made my way through the maze of trucks in Guild Street Goods Yard. At last I found the Deeside goods solemnly awaiting its trip into history. I boarded the brake van and, after a twenty minute delay, our engine, a Clayton No. D8610, the first on Deeside and probably the last, coupled up to our train and we made our way slowly out of the yard and accelerated out past Ferryhill on to the Great North metals.

We picked up speed steadily and after some fast running, we arrived at our first stop, Culter, where we picked up the travelling signalman and a young enthusiast who went on the footplate of the diesel. Our passengers aboard, we trundled slowly out of the station and began the climb through Drum, Park and Crathes. After some good running we glided down to Banchory, our second stop. There were two plate wagons carrying manure spreaders to be shunted into the deserted yard and this gave me ample time to photograph and to survey the layout. Banchory, once an important station, seemed only a shadow of its former self. However there are still traces of its past glory to be seen in the capacious passenger station with its large canopies and acetylene gas plant.

The next section of our journey I think was the most interesting of all. As we passed through the 'Brathens', just beyond Banchory, the rear of the brake van offered some magnificent views of the surrounding hills; views unknown to road travellers. After a slow climb to the summit of this section, we descended the long incline to Glassel at quite a considerable speed, as I remember having to hold on grimly to the rear of the van where I was standing. We kept up this terrific pace through Torphins but began to decelerate as we crossed the viaduct and rumbled through the 'Den' to tackle the stiff climb to Lumphanan.

On the other side of the summit we came to a halt at Auchlossan Crossing to enable the guard to open the 'gates' (two sets of two strands of barbed wire, each adorned with a piece of red cloth) which had been installed because the proper ones had been torn off by a train failing to brake in time the previous week. We passed through Dess and arrived at Aboyne where a van was shunted off. The local stationmaster joined us to make a last sentimental journey to Ballater.

After some smart running we reached the terminus half an hour ahead of schedule and were greeted by a crowd of about thirty who had turned out to see their 'trainie' for the last time. After some shunting operations and lunch, we glided out of Ballater to repeated blasts of the engine's horn — a poor substitute, I thought, for the shrill whistle of the Great North engine which I am sure would have been better appreciated on such an occasion.

We completed the return trip in fine style and I was surprised by the large turnout of enthusiasts on the lineside and by the lineside inhabitants who were out in force to wave us on our way for the last time. One hour early at 1545 we arrived at Clayhills Sidings and after saying my farewells to the guard and engine crew, I slipped slowly out of the yard with a headful of some wonderful memories of the Deeside railway.

(B. J. Ritchie in the Great North Review)

The Route Described

Deeside trains left the main line at Ferryhill Junction, $^1/_2$ mile south of the Joint Station, turning quite sharply west into the Dee valley. The first station for most of the life of the line was at Cults but for the duration of the 'Subby' service there were intermediate stations before there at Holburn Street, Ruthrieston and Pitfodels. Further suburban stations followed at West Cults, Bieldside, Murtle and Milltimber before reaching Culter. This was the terminus for the suburban trains but the town also boasted a flourishing paper mill with its own sidings and shunting engine or 'pug'.

From here on the railway was in open country and, as far as Banchory, never very far from the river, with stations at Drum and Park. The road connecting Park station with the South Deeside Road was built by the railway for the prime purpose of allowing residents on the other side of the river to use the trains. As the present day traveller will notice, it was also built like a railway and instead of following the ground surface it has embankments and cuttings! Because the road and bridge were private property the Company charged a toll which continued to be collected by BR until sometime in the 1950s when the charge per car was 3d (1.2p).

Crathes was originally a private halt for the Laird of Crathes but became a public station in 1863 when nearby Mills of Drum was closed.

Banchory was a large station as befitted the flourishing town it served. It was unusual in being lit by acetylene gas right up until it was closed. The gas was made in a small building which was always marked by a heap of white, spent carbide.

A short distance beyond Banchory, BR opened a platform in 1961 at Dee Street, a more convenient location for much of the town. The trains now turned away from the river and were faced with a stiff climb through woods and rough country for the following $2^1/_2$ miles. Next came Glassel serving a scattered population before arriving at Torphins. Further climbing followed over the Beltie Burn Viaduct and into 'Satan's Den' before the line dropped equally steeply through Lumphanan where direction changed again as the railway headed south-west back towards the Dee.

Leaving Aboyne station came a very short tunnel and then to Dinnet the railway was close to the road on one side and not far from the river on the other. Beyond that station it crossed a stretch of moorland before once again reaching the Dee at Cambus O'May.

This must surely be one of the most picturesque stations in the country perched as it is on a narrow shelf above the water. The adjoining suspension bridge was partly funded by the Great North and was used by travellers from the south side of the river to reach the station. It gradually fell into disrepair until in 1988 it was found to be cheaper to replace it with the present structure. The rebuilt bridge does not span the track to reach the road, as it did originally. An amus-

The 1905-built suspension bridge at Cambus O'May

ing condition about the funding of the first bridge was the prohibition of any kind of wheeled traffic, including bicycles, so turnstiles had to be maintained at the entrances.

On the final four miles to Ballater the hills rise quite sharply on the north side. As related earlier, the line had for a while continued on to Bridge of Gairn, hence the road bridge at the far end of the station.

The End of the Line

The very last train of all, the Culter goods, ran on 30th December 1966 and for once a sad occasion was graced with sunshine. In honour of the event the usual diesel was replaced by a Class B1 No. 61180 from Dundee which looked surprisingly clean as its black livery gleamed in the winter sun. Outward bound, the train, which left Guild Street at 10.40, consisted of four goods brake vans carrying some thirty people who had all purchased a First Class Ticket costing 6/6 (32^1/2p) for the return journey! Driver Frank Duncan had driven Deeside trains for the past 23 years and was glad to have a steam engine but the fireman, who had not handled a shovel for five years said his hands were feeling it. The guard, Bob Taylor, was another Deeside man.

The last ever train on the Deeside Line

It seems appropriate, considering the line's association with timber haulage that the final seven wagons lifted at Culter should contain timber destined for the railway works at Inverurie and Derby. The train then set off on its return journey.

At Ferryhill Junction the single line tablet was handed back to the signalman for the last time. The points were locked over for ever and 113 years, 3 months and 22 days of history came to an end.

What is Left?

Although the railway closed during 1966/67 track lifting did not take place for another four years, after which the formation lay derelict. Some years later, however, Aberdeen District Council created the Deeside Walkway between Duthie Park and Culter. This is a pleasant stroll and well worth a visit. It is also possible to walk some distance eastwards from Banchory. More recently a further walkway has been opened between Ballater and Cambus O'May while negotiations are well under way to continue this to Dinnet. Few people who use the attractive path through the oak woods below Craigendarroch at Ballater realise that it is the track bed of the abortive railway on to Braemar.

A number of stations survive. Pitfodels is now a house as are those at Murtle, Glassel and Dess. Cults is in use as a joiner's workshop while Park is used by a caravan dealer. Crathes is occupied by an engraver who is actively restoring the building. Aboyne, although now surrounded by tarmac, is owned by the Regional Council who let it out as shops. Dinnet is the local estate's office while Cambus O'May is another house. Ballater, owned by the District Council, is used as a restaurant, offices etc.

Banchory station has vanished without trace, although the old engine shed still stands as does the massive retaining wall built by the Great North to protect its property from the river. The station area is now a public park and it is hard to realise that once quite a large and imposing building ever existed here.

Torphins has also disappeared with the site now occupied by houses. Indeed the whole road layout has altered back to what it was before the railway came, with the road from Kincardine O'Neil to Inverurie once again having a clear run north from the square; although the diversionary road and bridge built when the station was made is still in use. The viaduct over the Beltie Burn has been demolished and its demise came as a nasty surprise to those working on it when it collapsed before expected to do so! Luckily no one was hurt.

Bus Services

So far this booklet has been about the railway, but a word about early bus services on Deeside is called for. The Great North of Scotland was one of the earliest railway companies to recognise the value of buses to act as feeders to its trains. The Company opened a number of routes, the first of which began running on 2nd May 1904 and connected Ballater with Braemar. This remained railway operated until 1930 when it was transferred to Messrs Alexanders, now Bluebird Buses, part of the Stagecoach group of companies. The bus depot and garage, behind the Invercauld Arms at Braemar, are still in use for their original purpose.

Three years later a summer only charabanc service began to run between Ballater and Strathdon as part of the inclusive rail/motor 'Three Rivers Tour' from Aberdeen back to Aberdeen via Deeside, the Lecht and Speyside. In those days the road over the Lecht was considered too steep and rough for motors so passengers transferred to a privately operated horse-drawn vehicle which took them to Tomintoul for an overnight stop. Next day they continued, again by charabanc, to Ballindalloch on Speyside where they transferred to a train for the return home via Craigellachie and Keith.

Envoi

Track lifting started on 6th April 1970 not far from Dess where an embankment had slipped, with the contractor working from Aboyne. Depending on ease of access, parts of the line were removed by rail to a place convenient for lorry access, while elsewhere the lorries ran along the track bed to the working site. The rails having been cut into short lengths were sent overseas as scrap metal. Progress was slow and the final stretch was not cleared until January 1971, a sad end to a fine railway. *R.I.P.*

Terminus: just beyond Ballater station

Opening and Closing Dates

	Miles	Opened	Closed	
			Passenger	Goods
Holburn Street	$1^1/_2$	2:7:1894	5:4:1937	—
Ruthrieston	$1^3/_4$	1856	5:4:1937	—
Pitfodels	3	2:7:1894	5:4:1937	—
Cults	$3^1/_2$	8:9:1853	28:2:1966	15:6:1964
West Cults	4	1:8:1894	5:4:1937	—
Bieldside	$4^3/_4$	1:6:1897	5:4:1937	—
Murtle	$5^1/_2$	8:9:1853	5:4:1937	5:4:1937
Milltimber	$6^1/_4$	1854	5:4:1937	5:4:1937
Culter	$7^1/_2$	8:9:1853	28:2:1966	2:1:1967
Drum	$9^3/_4$	1854	10:9:1951	10:9:1951
Park	$10^3/_4$	8:9:1853	28:2:1966	15:6:1964
Mills of Drum	13	8:9:1853	1:1:1863	—
Crathes	$14^1/_4$	8:9:1853	28:2:1966	15:6:1964
Banchory	$16^3/_4$	8:9:1853	28:2:1966	18:7:1966
Dee Street	$17^1/_2$	6:2:1961	28:2:1966	—
Glassel	$21^1/_2$	2:12:1859	28:2:1966	15:6:1964
Torphins	$23^3/_4$	2:12:1859	28:2:1966	29:3:1965
Lumphanan	27	2:12:1859	28:2:1966	15:6:1964
Dess	$29^1/_2$	2:12:1859	28:2:1966	1:7:1960
Aboyne	$32^1/_4$	2:12:1859	28:2:1966	18:7:1966
Dinnet	$36^1/_4$	17:10:1866	28:2:1966	15:6:1964
Cambus O'May	$39^1/_2$	1876	28:2:1966	—
Ballater	$43^1/_4$	17:10:1866	28:2:1966	18:7:1966

Bibliography

The Great North of Scotland Railway: *Vallance (revised edition1989)*

Regional History of the Railways of Great Britain — Vol.15 North of Scotland: *Thomas and Turnock(1989)*

The Great North of Scotland Railway: *Barclay-Harvey (1940)*

The Royal Deeside Line: *Farr (1968)*

Stories of Royal Deeside's Railway: *Farr (1971)*

The Old Deeside Road: *Fraser (1921) (reprinted 1980)*

The Great North Review *1964 to 1994 (quarterly)*

The Deeside Railway 1852-1866

Deeside Railway No.4 was built by Hawthorn of Leith in 1857 and the photo must date from before 1866 when the GNSR took over.

DEESIDE RAILWAY.

OPENING OF THE LINE FOR TRAFFIC.

ON and after THURSDAY the 8th SEPTEMBER, and until further notice, Trains will leave ABERDEEN and BANCHORY at the Hours undernoted:—

Departure from Aberdeen.

Miles.	TRAINS LEAVE	1. CLASSES 1 & 3.	2. CLASSES 1 & 3.	3. CLASSES 1 & 3.
	Aberdeen ....depart	7 0 A.M.	11·0 A.M.	4·39 P.M.
3¼	Cults	7·12 ,,	11·12 ,,	4·42 ,,
4¾	Murtle	7·18 ,,	11·18 ,,	4·48 ,,
7	Culter.................	7·26 ,,	11·26 ,,	4·56 ,,
10¼	Park	7·38 ,,	11·38 ,,	5·8 ,,
12¼	Mills of Drum	7·46 ,,	11·47 ,,	5·17 ,,
16¼	Banchory ....arrive	8·0 ,,	12·0 ,,	5·30 ,,

Arrivals in Aberdeen.

Miles.	TRAINS LEAVE	1. CLASSES 1 & 3.	2. CLASSES 1 & 3.	3. CLASSES 1 & 3.
	Banchory ....depart	8·30 A.M.	1·0 P.M.	6·30 P.M.
3¾	Mills of Drum	8·44 ,,	1·13 ,,	6·43 ,,
6	Park	8·53 ,,	1·22 ,,	6·52 ,,
9¼	Culter.................	9·5 ,,	1·34 ,,	7·4 ,,
11¼	Murtle	9·13 ,,	1·42 ,,	7·12 ,,
13	Cults	9·18 ,,	1·48 ,,	7·18 ,,
16¼	Aberdeen ....arrive	9·30 ,,	2·0 ,,	7·30 ,,

Newspaper advert for the opening of the line.

The Great North of Scotland Railway 1866 - 1922

The original Banchory station built by the Deeside Railway and opened in 1853. The gentleman in the top hat is no doubt the stationmaster, but just why are three young men standing one above the other on the ladder?

Banchory station was rebuilt in 1902 in a manner more in keeping with the town it served. This postcard view must have been taken shortly after completion.

Period piece at Culter. The GNSR bus is on the service to Midmar which only operated from June 1905 until November 1906.

Deeside train formed of six-wheeled carriages leaving Culter and heading towards Ballater.

Up Sunday 'King's Messenger' at Dinnet. The engine, No.105, belongs to Class T (LNER Class D41), twenty of which were built between 1895 and 1898.

A non-stop train from Aberdeen passes Cults. The station is now a joiner's workshop while the track is part of the Deeside Walkway from Duthie Park to Culter.

A goods train at Torphins station. Houses now occupy this site. An ornate vending machine stands on the far platform; similar looking machines appear at a few of the Deeside stations at this time.

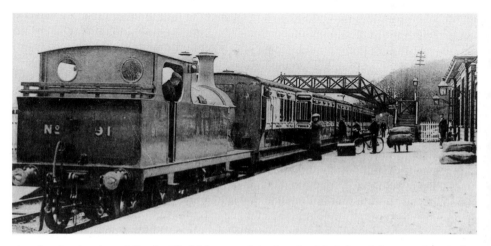

A suburban train at Murtle. No.91 is one of the batch of 0-4-4 tank locomotives built for suburban and branch line service.

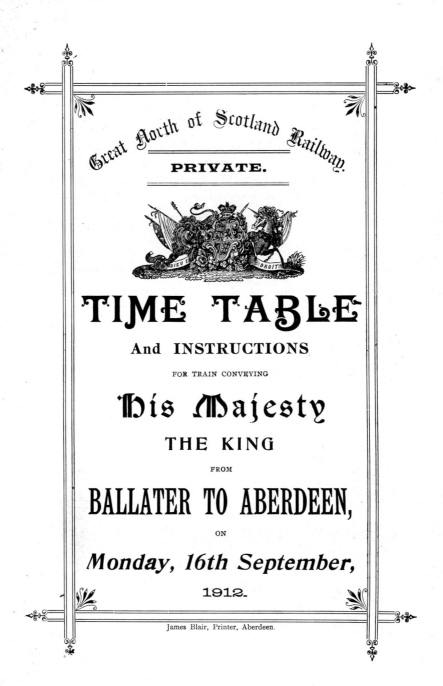

Great North of Scotland Railway.

PRIVATE.

TIME TABLE

And INSTRUCTIONS

FOR TRAIN CONVEYING

His Majesty

THE KING

FROM

BALLATER TO ABERDEEN,

ON

Monday, 16th September,

1912.

James Blair, Printer, Aberdeen.

Great North of Scotland Railway.

For Company's Servants only, and to be carefully read by them at the time they receive it.

NOTE.—*These Instructions must be kept strictly private, and must only be communicated to those Persons in the Service of the Company who in the discharge of their duty require to know and act upon them; and those Persons must not give any information to anyone respecting the hours or other arrangements set forth in these instructions.*

TIME TABLE AND INSTRUCTIONS

FOR TRAIN CONVEYING

His Majesty The King

From BALLATER to ABERDEEN

(En Route for Cambridge),

On MONDAY, 16th SEPTEMBER, 1912.

The ROYAL TRAIN will depart from, pass, and arrive at the various Stations as under:—

Distance. MILES.	STATIONS.	TIME. Arrive.	Pass.	Depart.
		P.M.	P.M.	P.M.
...	BALLATER, ...	...	...	7 20
3⅞	CAMBUS O'MAY, ...	...	7 27	...
6½	DINNET (cross 2·55 p.m. Down Train at Dinnet), ...	7 31	...	7 31
11	ABOYNE, ...	...	7 37	...
13¾	DESS, ...	...	7 41	...
16⅜	LUMPHANAN, ...	...	7 46	...
19½	TORPHINS (cross 6 40 p.m. Down Train at Torphins)	7 52	...	7 52
21⅞	GLASSEL, ...	...	7 55	...
26½	BANCHORY, ...	...	8 1	...
29	CRATHES.	...	8 5	...
32½	PARK, ...	...	8 9¾	...
33½	DRUM (cross 7·37 p.m. Down Train at Drum), ...	8 11	...	8 11
35⅞	CULTER	...	8 14	...
37	MILLTIMBER, ...	...	8 15½	...
37⅞	MURTLE, ...	...	8 17	...
38½	BIELDSIDE, ...	...	8 17¾	...
39⅛	WEST CULTS, ...	...	8 18½	...
39⅝	CULTS, ...	...	8 19	...
40¼	PITFODELS, ...	...	8 19¾	...
41½	RUTHRIESTON, ...	...	8 21½	...
41⅞	HOLBURN STREET, ...	...	8 22	...
42⅝	ABERDEEN—FERRYHILL JUNCTION, ...	8 25	...	8 30

NOTES OF WORKING.

ROYAL TRAIN.—The time of passing Intermediate Stations and of arrival at Aberdeen (Ferryhill Junction) must be strictly observed.

The Engine whistle is not to be sounded on approaching Signals or otherwise, except in emergency.

DOWN TRAINS.—The 2·55 p.m. Down Goods Train must arrive at Dinnet not later than 7·6 p.m., and is to remain there to cross the Royal Train, due to pass at 7·31 p.m.

The 6·40 p.m. Down Train must arrive at Torphins not later than 7·32 p.m., and is to remain there to cross the Royal Train, due to pass at 7·52 p.m.

The 7·37 p.m. Down Train must not pass Drum until the Royal Train, due at 8·11 p.m., has passed.

The 8·30 p.m. Down Train must not leave Aberdeen until the Royal Train has departed from Ferryhill Junction.

UP TRAIN.—The 8·10 p.m. Up Train must not start from Culter until the Royal Train has passed Murtle, nor pass Holburn Street until the Royal Train has departed from Ferryhill Junction.

The Engines of the Royal Train are to leave Ferryhill Junction at 8·32 p.m. for Aberdeen.

Instructions for Working.

1. To avoid all chance of detention, every Engine, Train, and Vehicle must be clear off and not allowed to proceed upon the Main Line between Ballater and Park for at least *Twenty minutes* before the time named in the Time Table for the passing of the Royal Train.

2. Every Engine, Train, and Vehicle must be clear off, and not allowed to proceed upon the Up Line between Park and Ferryhill Junction for at least *Twenty minutes* before the time named in the Time Bill for the passing of the Royal Train, and all Trains or Engines running upon the Down Line between Ferryhill Junction and Park must be slowed to a speed not exceeding *ten* miles an hour when meeting the Royal Train, on the Up Line, and must not whistle while passing it.

3. Guards of all Goods Trains standing or running upon Lines adjoining the Line upon which the Royal Train has to travel must carefully examine the loading of their Trains, and see that nothing is projecting or out of order.

4. Drivers of Trains standing in sidings or on adjoining Lines waiting for the passing of the Royal Train must prevent their Engines emitting smoke, or making a noise by blowing off steam, or whistling, when the Royal Train is passing.

5. The Station Master at each Station will see that the Signals are carefully attended to, and that all is made right for the Royal Train 20 minutes before it is timed to pass his Station.

6. Fifteen minutes before the Royal Train is timed to pass Stations provided with Telegraph Signal Instruments, the Signal " Is Line Clear " must be given to the Station in advance, and the Station in advance must if all is right immediately acknowledge the Signal, on receiving which acknowledgment the " All Right " Signals will be exhibited to allow the Royal Train to pass. If the " Is Line Clear " Signal is not taken by the Station in advance, the Royal Train is to be stopped by the Danger Signals being exhibited. Immediately the Royal Train has passed, the " Train entering Section " Signal must be sent to the Station in advance.

7. All Points over which the Royal Train will have to pass must be properly set, and all Facing Points securely clipped and padlocked by the Surfacemen, at least 20 minutes before the Royal Train is due, and until it has passed.

8. Station Masters must see that the Brakes of all Waggons in the Sidings are pinned down to prevent them moving, 20 minutes before the Royal Train is due.

9. Gatemen must lock their Gates at least 20 minutes before the Royal Train is due, and must not open them until it has passed ; and they must be very particular not to allow any obstruction at the Level Crossings. The Gates of Level Crossings, where there are no Gatekeepers, must be locked by the Surfacemen when walking over their Sections, half-an-hour at least before the Royal Train is due, and kept locked until it has passed, and at each Private Gate presently in use a " *Notice to Farmers* " must be posted up in a conspicuous position.

10. Surfacemen are to be posted along their lengths, so as to prevent the possibility of any impediment at the Occupation Road Crossings or upon any part of the Line, and must exhibit a Danger Signal when any obstruction exists. Each Surfaceman must examine his Section within at least half-an-hour of the time the Royal Train should pass over it.

11. The Guard in the front Van must keep his face towards the rear of the Train, and be constantly on the look-out on both sides of the Train to observe any Signals that may be given from any of the Guards or other attendants accompanying the Royal Train, and communicate instantly to the Driver any Signal he may receive.

12. The Signal for starting the Train must be given by the Guard in the front Van, but he must not give the authority for starting until after he has been verbally informed by the Carriage Superintendent that the examination of the Train is completed, and has exchanged Signals with the Guard in the rear Van, and also received intimation from the person in charge of the Station that all is right for the Royal Train to proceed, care being taken that all the members of the suite are seated before the Signal is given.

13. The Telegraph must be carefully watched during the time that the Royal Train is upon the Line. Messages connected with or affecting the passage of the Train must have precedence over all other messages.

14. The Telegraph Inspector will accompany the Train with a Portable Battery, which can be attached to the wires at any place in case of need—Should such be necessary, Call Signal will be Q.

15. All the Stations must be kept perfectly clear and private during the passage of the Royal Train, and no persons (excepting those properly authorised, the Company's Servants on duty, and the Police at those Stations where their services are required) are to be admitted to any of the Stations.

16. Every Officer of the Company must use the utmost care to insure the safe passage of the Royal Train over the Line.

Acknowledge Receipt to Passenger Superintendent.

ABERDEEN, *13th September,* 1912.

(350)

GEORGE DAVIDSON, General Manager.

The Royal Train will be fitted with the Westinghouse Brake, description and instructions for working of which see Appendix to Working Time Table.

An East Coast route Royal train crossing Dinnet Moor circa 1910.

West Coast Royal train near Banchory in early LNER days. (Note the children waving on the right.)

Nos. D6142 and D6145 take the empty stock to Ballater for the final Royal Train on 14th October 1965 which returned south after dark.

TIME TABLE

ARRANGED BY THE

GREAT NORTH OF SCOTLAND RAILWAY COMPANY,

FOR THE JOURNEY OF

HER MAJESTY'S

SERVANTS, HORSES, AND CARRIAGES,

FROM

BALLATER to WINDSOR,

ON

Tuesday, 20th, and Wednesday, 21st June, 1893.

	P.M.
Leave BALLATER, ...	5·55
Arrive ABERDEEN, ...	7·40
Leave Do., ...	7·55
Arrive PERTH, ...	10·55
Leave Do., ...	11·25
	A.M.
Arrive CARLISLE, ...	3·55
Leave Do., ...	4·10
Arrive PRESTON, ...	6·40
Leave Do., ...	6·45
Arrive BUSHBURY, ...	9·5
Leave Do., ...	9·15
Arrive OXFORD, ...	11·50
	P.M.
Leave Do., ...	12·20
Arrive WINDSOR, ...	1·55

Great North of Scotland Railway bus services

This Milnes-Daimler 18 seat bus was built in 1905 and ran for fifteen years. On this occasion it won through to the Invercauld Arms, Braemar, but it didn't always make it through severe winter snowdrifts on upper Deeside. The original conductor on the service wrote that, on some occasions, 'the conductor has had to carry the mails on horseback for a week on end.'

The scene could hardly be more different from that above! The link is that today's buses are still based at this building, the original GNS bus depot and garage in Braemar, built in 1904 behind the Invercauld Arms. *(Bluebird Buses)*

THE THREE RIVERS TOURS.

By Rail, Motor, and Coach, *via* the Dee, Don, and Spey, daily, from 1st July to 30th September.

TWO DAYS' TOUR—No. 1.

Aberdeen, Dinnet, Ballater, Strathdon, Corgarff, Tomintoul, Ballindalloch, Grantown.

From Aberdeen to Dinnet or Ballater by Rail ; thence by Motor Char-a-banc to Strathdon and Cockbridge (Corgarff) ; Coach to Tomintoul ; Motor Char-a-banc to Ballindalloch ; and Rail to Grantown and Aberdeen. The Route may be reversed.

Fares for the Round—20/- First Class ; 15/- Third Class.

Tickets for this Tour are issued at Edinburgh and Glasgow by the Caledonian and North British Railway Companies at the following Throughout Fares, viz. :—

	1st Class Rail, Motor, and Coach.	3rd Class Rail, Motor, and Coach.
Edinburgh (*via* Aberdeen in both directions), ...	55/	32/6
Edinburgh (*via* Aberdeen, returning *via* Boat of Garten and Dunkeld, or *vice versa*), ...	50/3 ...	31/3
Glasgow (*via* Aberdeen in both directions),... ...	58/3 ...	34/
Glasgow (*via* Aberdeen, returning *via* Boat of Garten and Dunkeld, or *vice versa*), ...	53/	32/6

TIME TABLE.

From Aberdeen to Deeside, Donside, and Speyside.

		A.M.
Aberdeen (Rail) ... ... dep.		8 5
Dinnet ,, ... arr.		9 30
		A.M.
Ballater (Motor) ... ... dep.		9 15
Dinnet ,, ... ,,		9 55
Strathdon (Newe Hotel) ,, ...		11 40
Do. do. ,, ... dep.		1 10p
Cockbridge (Allargue Hotel) ,, ... arr.		2 10
		P.M.
Cockbridge (Coach) ... ... dep.		2 45
Tomintoul ,, ... arr.		4 45

Next day.

	A.M.	P.M.
Tomintoul (Motor) ... ... dep.	8 30	2 0
Ballindalloch ,, ... ,, arr.	10 0	8 30
	A.M.	P.M.
Ballindalloch (Rail) ... ... dep.	10 13	3 41
Aberdeen ,, ... arr.	12p55	7 16

From Aberdeen to Speyside, Donside, and Deeside.

	A.M.	P.M.
Aberdeen (Rail) ... ... dep.	8 5	—
Ballindalloch ,, ... arr.	10 52	—
Grantown ,, ... dep.	9 48	3 18
	A.M.	P.M.
Ballindalloch (Motor) ... ... dep.	11 0	4 0
Tomintoul ,, ... arr.	12p40	5 40

Next day.

	A.M.	
Tomintoul (Coach) .. ... dep.	11 0	
Cockbridge (Allargue Hotel) ,, arr.	1 0p	
	P.M.	
Cockbridge (Motor) ... ... dep.	2 20	
Strathdon (Newe Hotel) ,, ... arr.	3 20	
Do. do. ,, ... dep.	3 30	
Dinnet (Motor) ... ... arr.	5 0	
Ballater ,, ... ,,	5 35	
	P.M.	P.M.
Ballater (Rail) ... ... dep.	5 50	7 30
Dinnet ,, ... ,,	6 3	7 43
Aberdeen ,, ... arr.	7 16	9 7

Circular Tickets are also issued at Edinburgh, Glasgow, and Aberdeen, for a Tour embracing the Spital of Glenshee, Braemar, and the above Tour. See the different Railway Companies' Tourist Programmes for particulars.

TWO DAYS' TOUR—No. 2.

Aberdeen, Alford, Strathdon, Corgarff, Tomintoul, Ballindalloch, Grantown.

Aberdeen to Alford by Rail ; thence by Motor to Strathdon and Cockbridge (Corgarff) ; Coach to Tomintoul ; Motor Char-a-banc to Ballindalloch ; and Rail to Grantown and Aberdeen. The Route may be reversed.

Fares for the Round—18/6 First Class ; 14/- Third Class.

Tickets for this Tour are issued at Edinburgh and Glasgow by the Caledonian and North British Railway Companies at the following Throughout Fares, viz. :—

	1st Class Rail, Motor, and Coach.	3rd Class Rail, Motor, and Coach.
Edinburgh (*via* Aberdeen in both directions), ...	53/6	31/6
Edinburgh (*via* Aberdeen, returning *via* Boat of Garten and Dunkeld, or *vice versa*), ...	48/9 ...	30/6
Glasgow (*via* Aberdeen in both directions),... ...	56/9 ...	33/
Glasgow (*via* Aberdeen, returning *via* Boat of Garten and Dunkeld, or *vice versa*), ...	51/6	31/9

OCTOBER, 1904.

80   GREAT NORTH OF SCOTLAND RAILWAY.

MOTOR OMNIBUS SERVICE BETWEEN BALLATER AND BRAEMAR.

	BALLATER TO BRAEMAR.	A.M.	P.M.	P.M.	
BY TRAIN.	Aberdeen, depart, ... ^ ...	8 5	12 20	5 35	...
	Culter, . ,, ...	8 19	12 34	5 48	...
	Banchory, ,, ...	8 43	1 0	6 11	..
	Torphins, ,, ...	9 0	1 15	6 26	...
	Aboyne, ,, ...	9 20	1 35	6 46	...
	Ballater, arrive, ...	9 45	2 0	7 10	...

		A.M.	P.M.	P.M.	
BY OMNIBUS.	Ballater Station, depart, ...	10 5	2 15	7 20	...
	Bridge of Gairn, ... ⎫				
	Abergeldie, ... ⎪				
	Crathie, ... ⎬ ...	*	*	*	...
	Invér, ... ⎪				
	Bridge of Dee, ... ⎭				
	Braemar (Invercauld Arms Hotel), arrive, ...	11 30	3 40	8 45	...
	Braemar (Fife Arms Hotel), ,, . ..	11 35	3 45	8 50	...

	BRAEMAR TO BALLATER.	A.M.	P.M.	P.M.	
BY OMNIBUS.	Braemar (Fife Arms Hotel), depart, ...	8 5	1 45	4 5	...
	Braemar (Invercauld Arms Hotel), depart, ...	8 10	1 50	4 10	...
	Bridge of Dee, ... ⎫				
	Inver, ... ⎪				
	Crathie, ... ⎬ ...	*	*	*	...
	Abergeldie, ... ⎪				
	Bridge of Gairn, ... ⎭				
	Ballater Station, arrive, ...	9 40	3 20	5 40	...

		A.M.	P.M.	P.M.	
BY TRAIN.	Ballater, depart, ...	9 55	3 35	6 0	...
	Aboyne, arrive, ...	10 16	3 56	6 21	...
	Torphins, ,, ...	10 35	4 16	6 41	...
	Banchory, ,, ...	10 47	4 28	6 53	...
	Culter, . ,, ...	11 10	4 53	7 15	...
	Aberdeen, ,, ...	11 30	5 15	7 35	...

* Provided seats are available, Passengers may join the Omnibus for or at any intermediate place on payment of Fares to be ascertained from the Conductor.

FARE.—BALLATER to BRAEMAR, or *vice versa*, 2/6.

TICKETS are issued on the Omnibus and should be retained until completion of the journey. Through tickets from Aberdeen to Braemar and *vice versa* are issued at the Booking Office at these places only.

SEATS may be booked beforehand on application at any of the Company's Stations and at the Booking Office, Braemar ; and to prevent disappointment early intimation should be given.

PASSENGERS' LUGGAGE.—Small hand luggage, under the Passenger's own care, carried free ; other luggage, not exceeding 1 cwt. each package, which can be conveyed without inconvenience, charged according to distance, size, and weight.

PARCELS.—Small parcels and packages charged according to distance, size, and weight.

BICYCLES, which can be carried without inconvenience, charged 1/- each.

N.B.—*The Company give notice that they do not undertake that the Omnibuses shall start or arrive at the times above specified ; nor will they be responsible for any loss, damage, or inconvenience which may arise from delay or detention.*

For further information apply to the Booking Clerks at Ballater and Braemar; to any of the Company's Stations ; or to Mr. W. DEUCHAR, Passenger Superintendent, Aberdeen.

Milnes-Daimler 'motor char-a-banc' of the type used on the Three Rivers Tour described in the facing timetable.

Durkopp 18 seat bus built in 1907 on the Ballater to Braemar service. When the service started , it had to overcome local reluctance to the loss of the four-in-hand summer stagecoach — complete with red-coated driver in tall grey hat and bugle.

London & North Eastern Railway 1923 - 1947

There are at least eleven well-filled coaches in this Banchory train as it leaves Aberdeen in charge of Class T (D41) No.6894. Judging by the heads hanging out of the windows it is probably an excursion.

The truly delightful setting of Cambus O'May alongside the river. The building is now a private house.

CHEAP FARES

From DRUM

EVERY DAY

(FROM 1st OCTOBER, 1937).

Return Tickets valid for return within Seven Days (Sundays not included)

To	Third Class Single		Third Class Return	
	s.	d.	s.	d.
*Aberdeen - - - - - - -	1	1	1	4
*Aboyne - - - - - - -	2	1	3	2
*Ballater - - - - - - -	2	11	4	2
*Banchory - - - - - - -	0	8½	1	1
‡Braemar - - - - - - -	4	7	7	2
*Cambus O' May - - - - - -	2	8	3	11
*Crathes - - - - - - -	0	4½	0	7½
*Culter - - - - - - - -	0	3½	0	6¼
*Cults - - - - - - - -	0	8½	1	1
*Dess - - - - - - - -	1	10	2	11
*Dinnet - - - - - - - -	2	8	3	8
*Glassel - - - - - - - -	1	3	1	7
*Lumphanan - - - - - - -	1	7	2	8
*Park - - - -, - - - -	0	2	0	4
*Torphins - - - - - - -	1	4	2	1

First Class Tickets are issued at 50 per cent. over the third class fare.

* Inward portions of Return Tickets to these stations are valid to return by Messrs. W. Alexander & Sons Motors, and Inward portions of Return Motor Tickets may be exchanged at Stations for return by Rail.

‡ Rail and Alexander's Motors.

CONDITIONS OF ISSUE.

Tickets at reduced fares (other than Day, Half-Day and Evening Tickets) are issued subject to the conditions of issue of ordinary passenger tickets, so far as applicable, as shown in the Company's Time Tables.

Children under 3 years of age, Free; 3 years and under 14, Half-Fare.

For Luggage Allowances also see Time Tables.

Aberdeen, September, 1937.

L·N·E·R

Henry Munro, Limited, Aberdeen.

N.S. 2717—500

Aboyne station in its hey-day. Looking towards Aberdeen.

The bridge at Park built by the GNS to provide access to the station for people living on the south side of the river. A charge was levied for the privilege of crossing, and the toll-keeper's house is seen on the left.

( )

Y 361 X

L·N·E·R

HALF-DAY EXCURSION

Milltimber

SATURDAY, 26th SEPTEMBER

FROM	Third Class Return Fare	FROM	Third Class Return Fare
Inverurie	2/-	Kintore } Kinaldie }	1/9

OUTWARD JOURNEY				RETURN JOURNEY						
		a.m.	a.m.			p.m.	p.m.	p.m.	p.m.	p.m
Inverurie - dep.		11·34	11·50	Milltimber	dep.	5·10	5·47	6·32	8·10	10 27
Kintore - ,,		11·41	...	Aberdeen	arr.	5·30	6· 7	6·52	8·30	10·47
Kinaldie - ,,		11·47	...	Aberdeen	dep.	5·55	6·50	7·25	9·20	9·40	11·20
Aberdeen - arr.		12· 5p	12·17p	Kinaldie -	arr.	6·23	...	...	9·47	10· 4	11·47
Aberdeen - dep.		12·30	1· 5	Kintore -	,,	6·30	...	...	9·54	10·11	11·54
Milltimber - arr.		12·48	1·23	Inverurie -	,,	6·39	7·19	7·51	10· 0	10·18	12· 0

Conditions of Issue of Excursion Tickets and other Reduced Fare Tickets.

Excursion Tickets and Tickets at Fares less than the ordinary fares are issued subject to the Notices and Conditions in the Company's current Time Tables.

Children under three years of age, Free ; three years and under fourteen, Half Fares.

For Luggage Allowances also see Time Tables.

Special Attraction :

BOY SCOUTS' RALLY AT MILLTIMBER

Aberdeen, September, 1936.

James Blair, 24 Market Street, Aberdeen.   N.S. 2109—750

British Railways 1948 - 1966

Up Aberdeen train at Torphins in the early 1950s. No.62275 'Sir David Stewart' was named after the GNSR chairman in office when the Class F engines, the last built for the company, were ordered in 1919.

Culter Paper Mill's 'pug' was built by Messrs Peckett, Bristol in 1941 and bought second hand in 1954. It was the second such engine owned by the mill.

The 3.18pm train to Ballater, seen here near Glassel, is in the charge of Class B12 No.61508. Although taken on 13th April 1954 the engine is still in LNER green livery. The coaches are also former LNER vehicles, but carry British Railway's crimson and cream livery.

Goods train arriving at Ballater with BR Standard tank 2-6-4T No.80005 in May 1954. The sun-dappled hills in the background are a reminder of the line's scenic beauty.

BRITISH RAILWAYS

B. 29543

ABOYNE
HIGHLAND GAMES

Excursions
To Aboyne

WEDNESDAY,
7th SEPTEMBER, 1960

OUTWARD					RETURN				
	a.m.	a.m.	a.m.	p.m.		p.m.	p.m.	p.m.	p.m.
Aberdeen leave	8 12	9 40	10 15	12 45	Aboyne - leave	5 30	5 52	7 20	8 22
Cults- - ,,	8 20	9 48	10 24	12 54	Dess - arrive	...	...	7 25	...
Culter - ,,	8 29	9 55	10 30	1 0	Lumphanan ,,	5 40	6 2	7 32	8 32
Park - - ,,	8 37	10 2	10 38	....	Torphins - ,,	5 48	6 9	7 39	8 39
Crathes - ,,	8 42	10 7	10 44		Glassel - ,,	...	...	7 44	...
Banchory - ,,	8 48	10 13	10 50	1 18	Banchory - ,,	6 0	6 19	7 52	8 49
Glassel - ,,	8 56	10 21	11 4	1 27	Crathes - ,,	6 6	...	...	...
Torphins - ,,	9 1	10 26	11 11	1 34	Park - - ,,	6 14	6 28	...	...
Lumphanan ,,	9 8	10 33	11 19	1 42	Culter - ,,	6 21	6 37	8 13	...
Dess - - ,,	9 12	10 37	11 24	1 47	Cults - - ,,	...	...	8 19	...
Aboyne - arrive	9 17	10 42	11 30	1 53	Aberdeen - ,,	6 38	6 49	8 27	9 16

SECOND CLASS RETURN FARES FROM

Aberdeen	Banchory	Crathes	Cults	Culter
5/6	**2/6**	**3/9**	**5/6**	**4/11**
Dess	Glassel	Lumphanan	Park	Torphins
1/-	**2/2**	**1/6**	**4/8**	**1/11**

OUTWARD			RETURN			
	a.m.	p.m.		p.m.	p.m.	p.m.
Ballater leave	10 3	12 30	Aboyne leave	4 27	7 9	9 37
Dinnet ,,	10 14	12 41	Dinnet arrive	4 35	7 17	9 45
Aboyne arrive	10 21	12 48	Ballater ,,	4 45	7 27	9 56

SECOND CLASS RETURN FARES FROM

Ballater	Dinnet
2/4	**1/3**

TICKETS OBTAINABLE IN ADVANCE

at Stations and accredited Rail Ticket Agencies and are valid on the date for which issued and by the trains specified.

Children under three years of age free; three years and under fourteen, half-fare.

All information regarding Excursions and Cheap Fares will be supplied on application at Stations or to J. H. Young, District Traffic Superintendent, 80 Guild Street, Aberdeen, Telephone 23432.

NOTICE AS TO CONDITIONS.—These tickets are issued subject to the British Transport Commission's published Regulations and Conditions applicable to British Railways exhibited at their Stations or obtainable free of charge at station ticket offices.

BR 35000—BF—August, 1960   Blairs (Printers) Ltd., Aberdeen.

A Cravens-built DMU rolls into Dess on its trip towards Aberdeen.

Goods train passing the site of Ruthrieston station in February 1960 headed by an English Electric Type 1 engine No.D8028. *(A. Edward)*

BR Class 4 2-6-0 N0.76107 coasts into Dinnet on an up train from Ballater. The empty platforms — even by Deeside standards — are a clear signal of danger ahead for the whole line.

A fine spring day at Ballater sees the battery railcar sitting in front of some of the spare carriages which were kept at the terminus. The date is May 1960.

Table 40

Table 40 — **ABERDEEN and BALLATER**

Miles	Week Days only	am	am	pm E	pm S	pm	pm	pm (Runs until 8th October, 1964 and from 26th April, 1965)	pm F (Runs 9th October, 1964 to 24th April, 1965)
—	**Aberdeen** dep	8 9	9 38	1 55	1 55	3 45	6 10	8 35	8 35
3¾	Cults	8 17	9 46	...	...	3 53	6 18	...	...
7½	Culter	8 27	9 53	2 8	2 8	4 0	6 25	..	..
10¾	Park	8 34	10 0	2 15	2 15	4 7	6 32	...	...
14	Crathes	8 39	10 5	..	..	4 12	..	..	..
17	Banchory	8 45	10 11	2 25	2 25	4 22	6 42	9 10	9 10
17½	Dee Street Halt	8 47	10 13	2 27	2 27	4 24	6 44	9 12	9 12
21½	Glassel	8 56	10 22	2K36	2 36	4 33	6 53	9K20	9K20
23¾	Torphins	9 1	10 27	2 41	2 41	4 38	6 58	9 25	9 25
27	Lumphanan	9 8	10 34	2 48	2 48	4 45	7 5	9 32	9 32
29⅓	Dess	9 12	10 38	..	2 52	4 49	7 9	..	..
32¼	Aboyne	9 17	10 43	2 56	2 57	4 54	7 14	9 40	9 40
36¾	Dinnet	9 25	10 51	3 4	3 5	5 2	7 22	9 48	9 48
39¼	Cambus o'May Halt	9K31	10K57	...	...	...	7K28	..	...
43¼	**Ballater** arr	9 37	11 3	3 14	3 15	5 12	7 34	9 58	9 58

Miles	Week Days only	am	am	pm	pm	pm	pm F (Runs 9th October, 1964 to 24th April, 1965)	pm (Runs until 8th October, 1964 and from 26th April, 1965)
—	**Ballater** dep	7 20	10 3	12 30	3 25	5 33	8 3	8 3
3¾	Cambus o'May Halt	7K27	10K10	12K37	3K32	...	...	...
6½	Dinnet	7 31	10 14	12 41	3 36	5 43	8 13	8 13
11	Aboyne	7 38	10 21	12 48	3 43	5 50	8 20	8 20
13¾	Dess	7 43	10 26	12 53	3 48	..	..	..
16¼	Lumphanan	7 48	10C36	12 58	3 53	6 0	8 30	8 30
19¾	Torphins	7 55	10 43	1 5	4 0	6 7	8 37	8 37
21¾	Glassel	8 0	10 48	1K10	4 5	6 12	...	...
25¾	Dee Street Halt	8 7	10 55	1 17	4 12	6 19	8 47	8 47
26¼	Banchory	8 9	10 57	1 19	4C20	6 21	8 49	8 49
29¼	Crathes	8 14	11 2	..	4 25	..	..	..
32¼	Park	8 19	11 7	1 28	4 30	6 33	...	...
35¾	Culter	8 25	11 13	1 34	4 36	6 39	9 3	9 3
39⅓	Cults	8 31	11 19	...	4 42	...	...	...
43¼	**Aberdeen** arr	8 39	11 27	1 46	4 50	6 51	9 15	9 15

C Arr 6 minutes earlier
E Except Saturdays
F Fridays and Saturdays only

K Calls to set down on request to guard or when there are passengers to be taken up

S Saturdays only

PARTIES OF EIGHT

Parties of eight or more adults, travelling together in each direction, can, by prior arrangement with British Railways, obtain second class tickets at reduced fares. Party travel tickets are issued to cover a journey between any two points and are valid only on the day of issue. When possible, accommodation in trains will be reserved without additional charge. Further information may be obtained at British Railways stations or agencies.

One of the final timetables.

The last passenger train to Aberdeen is given a fine send-off from the folk of Ballater on the night of Saturday 26th February, 1966. *(A.R. Forsyth)*

Private contractors Arnott Young Ltd lifted the Deeside line mainly by rail, using two elderly diesel locomotives. Here one is at work in Aboyne station.